BOOK ANALYSIS

Written by Fanny Normand
Translated by Rebecca Neal

AF 131346

Nadja

BY ANDRÉ BRETON

Bright
≡Summaries.com

ANDRÉ BRETON

FRENCH SURREALIST WRITER

- **Born in Tinchebray, France in 1896.**
- **Died in Paris in 1966.**
- **Notable works:**
  - *The Magnetic Fields* (1920), book written with Philippe Soupault
  - *Nadja* (1928), novel
  - *Mad Love* (1937), novel

André Breton was born in Tinchebray, northwest France in 1896. He was a novelist, poet and essayist, and is best known for founding the Surrealist movement. In 1919, he created the review *Littérature* with his friends Philippe Soupault and Louis Aragon, in which he published the first ever Surrealist text, *The Magnetic Fields*. In 1924, he published the *Surrealist Manifesto*, which made him the de facto leader of the movement. Breton, who also wrote *Nadja* and *Mad Love*, was a member of the French Communist Party between 1927 and 1935. He died in Paris in 1966.

NADJA

THE SURREALIST EPIC

- **Genre:** novel
- **Reference edition:** Breton, A. (1999) *Nadja*. Trans. Howard, R. London: Penguin.
- **1ˢᵗ edition:** 1928
- **Themes:** meeting, Surrealism, beauty, literature

Nadja is an autobiographical novel by André Breton which was first published in 1928. The central part of the book recounts the author's meeting with Nadja, who he saw for nine days between 4 and 12 October 1926 in Paris.

He began writing the book in August 1927, while he was on holiday in Normandy. The following autumn, when he was back in Paris, he added illustrations. In November, he read the first part of *Nadja* to his Surrealist friends. At this time, he met Suzanne Muzard, and went to the south of France with her for two weeks. In December, he added a third part to *Nadja*, which is partly dedicated to Muzard. The book was first published in 1928, before being altered again in 1963.

SUMMARY

Nadja initially comprised three distinct parts, which all revolve around a central element: the encounter with the young woman of the title. It is not clear where one part ends and the next begins, as they are broken up only by a blank space.

PROLOGUE

In the prologue, which Breton wrote when the book was republished in 1963, he explains why he felt the need to improve his work 35 years after it first appeared. Specifically, he wanted to express himself better by finding more suitable terms and writing more fluidly.

ELUSIVE REALITY

The first part of the book is a theoretical reflection on literature and on the arts in general. Breton's intention is to overturn literary conventions.

He begins by asking himself "Who am I?", then immediately reformulates the question to refer to "whom I 'haunt'". Breton says that his true self constantly escapes him and that he cannot tell the truth about his life: he is condemned to give a representation of it that is nothing more than an unsatisfying mental reconstruction. For him, the important thing is to try to stand out from other people: he wants to find what makes him unique.

Breton thinks that books are not enough to express the uniqueness of their author, as they are only a reflection of this uniqueness. This is why, in his view, literary criticism should pay more attention to the minor events of everyday life: it is through these little details that a writer's personality is revealed.

Finally, Breton questions himself about the way the world can be perceived, and explains that a person's state of mind when they perceive things is more important than the way of perceiving them. In other words, it is less important to say what we see than to say how we look. Breton compares himself to Huysmans (French writer, 1848-1907) by recognising that Huysmans was able to show that appearance and the things that can be expressed conceal a dynamic of mysterious forces and powers that the writer must uncover and reveal to the reader. Where so many other writers try to reproduce reality in their books, Huysmans takes literature in a different direction: he does not depict the seemingly understandable parts of life, but the parts that cannot be grasped.

By proposing to recount the smallest coincidences, generate random associations of ideas, no matter how strange they may be, and make comparisons that are usually not made, the narrator aims to discover the other side of life explored by Huysmans, in the firm conviction that reality is more than what we normally say about it. To do this, he plans to use automatic writing (an approach which involves writing down literally everything that comes to mind). To tell the story of his relationship with Nadja, he therefore lets his pen move freely and uncover the chance comparisons where life is hidden. Breton adds that the account he is preparing to write may end up deforming or drastically reducing the reality of his and Nadja's story. However, this is not a problem, because he is not trying to recount minor incidents, but rather to give words to things that do not already have them. Nonetheless, this does not mean that he is turning his back on reality. For example, he sets the start of his story at the Panthéon in Paris, which really exists.

THE PRECURSORS TO THE ENCOUNTER

The story begins at the Hotel des Hommes, Place du Panthéon, in 1918. Breton describes some memorable encounters, the places he visited between 1918 and 1927, and the effect that certain objects and some of his dreams have on him, among other things, before discussing the first time he met Nadja. He emphasises the unsettling coincidences that he observed, although he never attempts to interpret them. Later, he and the reader come to understand that this series of coincidences in fact heralded his meeting with Nadja; this meeting itself presages what he calls "the Marvel".

Breton then recounts the week or so he spent with Nadja in the form of a diary, dated 5 to 12 October. The narrative then shifts to the present. During these few days, he walks the streets of Paris with her. They go to a café, where she talks to him about her childhood and confesses that she had to work as a prostitute in order to survive.

Breton is fascinated by the resemblance he sees between

the young woman's behaviour and Surrealism, even though she does not yet know anything about the literary movement. He gets her to read some Surrealist texts, and she is particularly moved by some of them. However, he very quickly begins to have his doubts about their relationship and realises that he cannot love her ("It is unforgivable of me to go on seeing her if I do not love her. Don't I love her?"). The diary breaks off on 12 October, after he has described a trip to Saint-Germain.

In the pages that follow, Breton tries to understand his relationship with Nadja. To do this, he first remembers some of the things she said and drew, which he carefully describes (in particular "The Lovers' Flower", a drawing reproduced on p. 117), then the objects which inspired reflections in the young woman. All he does is describe: he does not suggest any interpretation, and rejects all psychological analysis.

Several months after they first met, Breton tells us that he has learnt that Nadja has been committed to a psychiatric hospital. He cannot help feeling guilty, as he thinks that he might have helped develop her penchant for wild ideas.

BEAUTY

In the epilogue to *Nadja*, Breton talks about what has happened in his life since he finished writing the first two parts of the text. He explains that he now feels an intense emotion that affects his heart more than his mind. The time when he met Nadja already seems to belong to the distant past.

He then explains that he is not satisfied with the illustrated part of his text. Now that he is rereading it several months later, he feels that the photographs do not match his memories.

Next, Breton addresses an anonymous "You". This is Suzanne Muzard, who he met in 1927, when he had already written the first parts of the book.

The last part of the epilogue is an homage to beauty, which, in his view, should not be static or dynamic, but made up of "jolts and shocks". He then transcribes a story from a newspaper: a plane that is about to crash sends a final message saying that it is near an island called the Ile du Sable. The book ends with a sentence which returns to the idea of beauty made up of "jolts and shocks": "Beauty will be CONVULSIVE or will not be at all."

CHARACTER STUDY

The term "character" does not really apply to *Nadja*, insofar as Breton is describing an episode in his life. This means that all the characters are people who really existed.

ANDRÉ BRETON

When Breton meets Nadja in October 1926, he is 31. He is the leader of the Surrealist movement, and already has a certain degree of fame thanks to the *Surrealist Manifesto*. Before he meets Nadja for the first time, he notices a series of "petrifying coincidences", which he recounts in the first part of the book. According to him, these coincidences heralded his encounter with the young woman.

When he sees Nadja in the street, he is immediately struck by her appearance: she is "so delicate she scarcely seemed to touch the ground as she walked", and she has a "faint smile" and "magnificent eyes". They see each other every day for a week. He likes the fact that she is particularly receptive to Surrealist texts. However, on 7 October, he begins to have his doubts about their relationship and ends up drifting away from her for good.

NADJA

Léona D. was born in Lille in May 1902. After giving birth to a daughter, she went to Paris in 1923. She lived on the margins of society, and made a living through prostitution and drug trafficking. When she meets Breton, she is quick to bring up her money problems ("She mentioned the financial difficulties she was having, even insisted on them, but apparently as a way of explaining the wretchedness of her appearance").

She makes an effort to read Surrealist works and seems particularly moved when she reads a poem by Alfred Jarry. In many respects, she seems to be the embodiment of Surrealism.

On 21 March 1927, she is committed to a hospital "after the eccentricities in which it seems she had indulged herself in the hallways of her hotel". She is later moved to another psychiatric institution near Lille, where she remains until her death on 15 January 1941.

"YOU"

The mysterious young woman who Breton evokes in the epilogue to *Nadja* is Suzanne Muzard, who he fell in love with in November 1927. The couple went to the south of France together; this journey is described at the end of the book. With hindsight, Breton realises that meeting Nadja simply foreshadowed this relationship: "Without doing it on purpose, you have taken the place of the forms most familiar to me, as well as several figures of my foreboding. Nadja was one of these last, and it is just that you should have hidden her from me".

ANALYSIS

The movement

In 1921, Breton, who was increasingly interested in theories on the subconscious, discovered Freud. He and his friends then began experimenting with automatic writing (meaning spontaneous writing, without reflection, morality or reasoning interrupting the act), accounts of dreams and writing under hypnosis, as he saw these methods as the best way of exploring the subconscious. This exploration was above all conceived as a way of freeing the mind and getting to know man better, especially the things he tends to repress. These writing techniques soon became the hallmark of the Surrealist movement, which became official in 1924 when Breton published the *Surrealist Manifesto*.

Surrealism is characterised not only by a desire to reveal the subconscious, but also by a rebellion against the cultural values of the time and the system of morality and institutions that led to the disaster of the First World War.

The group came to an end in 1969, after all of its main members had died.

Nadja: a Surrealist manifesto

The *Surrealist Manifesto* was the founding text of Surrealism and set out the features of this school. *Nadja*, which was published a few years later, is more than an illustration of these precepts: for several reasons, this text can be considered a manifesto of Surrealism in its own right. It both illustrates and advocates:

- The exaltation of freedom. Breton condemns the excesses of reason and social conformism, which he sees as obstacles to freedom ("human emancipation in every respect [...] remains the only cause worth serving"). For him, logic and reason are "the most hateful of prisons".
- A Surrealist use of language. In *Manifestoes of Surrealism*, which sets out the main ideas of the movement, Breton wrote that "Language has been given to man so that he may make Surrealist use of it" (1969: 32). He illustrates this in *Nadja*, where he tries to use original images and unexpected word associations to disrupt the mechanisms of thought and change his readers' perceptions of reality. For example, he evokes Nadja's "fern-colored eyes" and regularly uses popular expressions or proverbs but distorts their meaning. It is also worth noting that Breton's sentences are generally dense, convoluted, complex and, above all, loaded with references and symbols. They aim to reveal the author's thought process and reproduce the complexity of reality. Breton seeks above all to free language in order to free thought.
- The use of photographs. Breton tells the reader that he is trying to eliminate all descriptions: in their place, he inserts photographs of places into his text. Descriptions are rejected because they reproduce reality: since the Surrealists are trying to express the inexpressible, descriptions no longer have any value. However, these illustrations do not mean that Breton never gives us

more detailed descriptions, but these always aim to look deeper into the other side of reality. For example, as well as the photograph representing the shop Bois-Charbons (p. 29), he describes the round wood of the sign which made him hallucinate.

- The reproduction of Nadja's drawings. As these images come from the young woman's mind, their reproduction in the book is an integral part of the Surrealist approach, which tries to gain access to the subconscious. These drawings are surprising above all because of their density and symbolism, which Breton tries to explain in minute detail in his text. However, some of these drawings are still a complete mystery; even Nadja does not know why there is a mask in the bottom left-hand corner of one of them. Whatever the reason, these drawings reveal Nadja's highly developed Surrealist sensibility.

Nadja: an embodiment of Surrealism

When Breton and Nadja meet, the young woman knows nothing about Surrealism, so he introduces her to some texts. She quickly reveals a high degree of appreciation for these writings, but the affinity between Nadja and Surrealism goes even further. Through her way of living, her attitudes and her way of expressing herself, she embodies the entire Surrealist project:

- Like Breton, Nadja is characterised by her openness to events.
- She sees life as a game. The day they meet, she asks Breton to play a game which involves improvising stories as spontaneously as possible, and tells him that this is

how she lives.

- She is free and does not follow social conventions. When Breton asks her where she has dinner, she responds: "'Where?' (pointing): 'oh, over there, or there (the two nearest restaurants), wherever I happen to be, you know."
- She appreciates analogies and tries to identify disconcerting links. For example, on 6 October she points out that they have gone from the Place Dauphine to a bar called La Dauphin.
- She produces drawings which feature many symbols that sometimes even she cannot explain. For example, she does not know what the mask she drew in the corner of one picture means. She puts herself in the same position as a Surrealist trying their hand at automatic writing: her drawings are dictated by her subconscious, and she draws spontaneously and often mysteriously.
- Like Breton, she makes unexpected word associations in order to free language from its restrictive logic. He remembers some of the phrases she came up with, such as "The lion's claw embraces the vine's breast".
- Finally, she illustrates the theme of madness, while the Surrealists prioritise imagination. In the *Surrealist Manifesto*, Breton had discussed his fascination with madness. Nadja proves unable to adapt to reality and is a victim of her imagination, which causes her to be committed to a psychiatric hospital.

Mutual fascination

From the first time they meet, Nadja and Breton both seem to recognise themselves in the other person. While he is fascinated by the young woman's appearance, her attraction to him is of a different kind. On numerous occasions, she compares him to a master or to the sun. She worships him like a god, and regularly talks about his power over her: "You are my master. I am only an atom respiring at the corner of your lips or expiring".

Breton's fascination with Nadja is above all intellectual: he is attracted to her because she seems to embody Surrealism. At the same time, however, she tries to match up to his image of her, for example by identifying herself with the women he evokes in his stories, or with real or mythical characters.

However, Breton quickly realises that she is completely submissive to him ("it is apparent that she is at my mercy"), which is why he cannot feel the same love that she feels for him, and that he will later feel for another woman.

Breton's guilt

While writing *Nadja*, Breton cannot help feeling guilty, as he believes that he is partially responsible for the young woman's confinement. First of all, he admonishes himself for not feeling the same love that she felt for him, which could have prevented "the fatal result". Next, he fears that he put her on the path to madness: she held on to "that idea she had always had but in which I had only too warmly encouraged her, which I had only too readily aided her in giving supremacy over all the rest, the idea that freedom [...] must be enjoyed as unrestrictedly as it is granted".

The sign of the marvel

Nadja's appearance in Breton's life followed on from the precursors which he tries to decipher in the first part of the book. For example, the young woman had been heralded by other women he had met on his way, such as Fanny Beznos, the bookseller at the Saint-Ouen flea-market, and the actress Blanche Derval.

However, in 1927, when Breton meets Suzanne Muzard and falls madly in love with her, he realises that Nadja was nothing more than the forerunner of the "mysterious, improbably, unique, bewildering and certain love" embodied by the "You'" who Breton addresses in the epilogue. From then on, he no longer feels the need to continue searching for his identity, as represented by the opening question "Who am I?". The "You" he is talking to has put an end to "this succession of terrible or charming enigmas".

THE SEARCH FOR IDENTITY AND COINCIDENCES

To get to know himself and succeed in his search for identity introduced by the opening question "Who am I?", Breton does not try to explore his psychology and inner life, but attempts to interpret a series of mysterious coincidences, which he sees as signals, the only things that can reveal to him what makes him different from other men. Consequently, at the beginning of the book he analyses the various episodes of his life before he met Nadja. He has the impression that he is not the only one controlling his life: there are "facts which may belong to the order of pure observation, but which on each occasion present all the appearances of a signal [...] which convince me of my error in occasionally presuming that I stand at the helm alone".

This is why he claims to be open to events. This openness can be seen in particular through his wanderings. In a world in which everything can resonate with other things and analogies and coincidences are a frequent occurrence, we must remain alert if we want to explore and understand life. In particular, he writes that "Perhaps life needs to be deciphered like a cryptogram".

FURTHER REFLECTION

SOME QUESTIONS TO THINK ABOUT...

- What is the role of chance in the story? Discuss, with the help of examples.
- Can *Nadja* truly be described as a novel? Explain your answer.
- In Breton's diary about his encounters with Nadja, is it possible to detect signs of her future madness in her behaviour?
- Why can Nadja's drawings be described as Surrealist? Explain your answer.
- At the start of the book, Breton explains that his work follows two anti-literary principles: the inclusion of photographs and the tone adopted, which is similar to that of medical observation. Explain and comment on this.
- In your opinion, why does Breton consider his relationship with Nadja to be a failure?
- In your opinion, how does the series of coincidences that Breton evokes at the start of the book pave the way for Nadja's entrance?
- "Beauty will be CONVULSIVE or will not be at all." Comment on this statement.
- What is the status and the role of the imagination, for the Surrealists and in this text?
- Analyse how Nadja and Breton are represented in the young woman's drawings. What conclusions can you draw from this?
- In your opinion, can this text be described as an autobiography?

We want to hear from you!
Leave a comment on your online library
and share your favourite books on social media!

FURTHER READING

REFERENCE EDITION

- Breton, A. (1999) *Nadja*. Trans. Howard, R. London: Penguin.

REFERENCE STUDIES

- Breton, A. (1969) *Manifestoes of Surrealism*. Trans. Seaver, R. and Lane, H.R. Ann Arbor: University of Michigan Press.
- Polizzotti, M. (2008) *Revolution of the Mind: The Life of André Breton*. Boston: Black Widow Press.

www.brightsummaries.com

Ebook EAN: 9782806295897

Paperback EAN: 9782806298492

Legal Deposit: D/2017/12603/328

Cover: © Primento

Digital conception by Primento, the digital partner of publishers.